The OLYMPIC GAMES
Trivia Book

Copyright Jenine Zimmers ©2023

What you need

- This book!
- 2-6 players
- Scoring method (Pen and paper, or smartphone)

How to play

Choose a person to keep score.

General trivia questions are worth 1, 2 or 3 points based on difficulty. The youngest player reads the first question to the player directly to his or her right. If the player answers correctly, he or she earns the number of points for that question. (Correct answers can be found on the page that follows each question.) The youngest player passes the book to the person on his or her left, who then asks the next question to the youngest player. Continue moving the book around your group in this fashion.

If only two players, simply pass the book back and forth. You may also choose to play in two teams instead of as individuals.

If a player lands on a bonus round page, that person or team will have an opportunity to earn up to 10 points. Read all instructions aloud when landing on a bonus round page. The question reader should keep track of correct answers in a bonus round, and tally the points for the scorekeeper.

The player or team with the most points at the end wins. You may choose to play the entire book. For a shorter round, elect to end the game on page 50 or page 100, and pick up from there next time.

QUESTION

In which country did the Olympics originate?

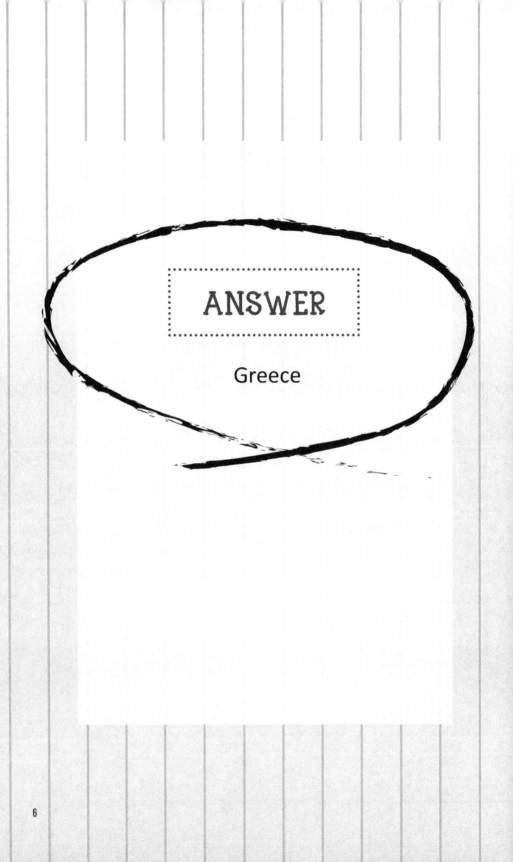

QUESTION

At the 2012 Olympics, who became the youngest swimmer to win gold in the women's 800-meter freestyle?

ANSWER

Katie Ledecky (United States). She has won seven Olympic golds total and 19 world championship gold medals, both of which are a record in women's swimming.

QUESTION

In what year could the Olympic Games be viewed on mobile devices for the first time?

ANSWER

2006

2 POINTS

QUESTION

Track and field Olympians Jesse Owens and Carl Lewis both won gold in the 100-meter, the 200-meter, the 4x100-meter relay and what other event?

ANSWER

The long jump

QUESTION

What is the lowest-populated country to win a medal at the Summer Olympic Games?

ANSWER

Bermuda

QUESTION

Who was the first Black athlete to win gold in the Winter Olympics?

ANSWER

Vonetta Flowers

QUESTION

Figure skating and what other sport were originally part of the Summer Olympics?

ANSWER

Ice hockey

QUESTION

In what year were the first modern Olympics held?

ANSWER

1896

QUESTION

Sprinter Wilma Rudolph, the first American woman to win three gold medals in a single Olympics, overcame the loss of strength in her left leg and foot after contracting what disease at age 5?

ANSWER

Polio

BONUS Round!

BONUS Round!

Four new sports debuted at the 2021 Olympic Games in Tokyo.
Name them. You may take four guesses total.
(Two points per correct answer for a maximum of 8 points.)

Skateboarding

Surfing

Climbing

Karate

QUESTION

The official motto of the Olympics is "Citius, Altius, Fortius." What does it mean in English?

ANSWER

"Faster, Higher, Stronger"

QUESTION

What Jamaican sprinter won eight gold Olympic medals and often performed his famous "Lightning Bolt" celebration after victory?

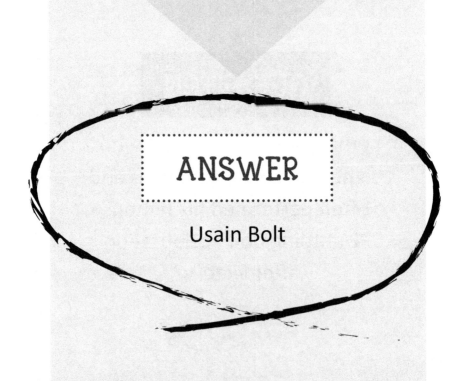

ANSWER

Usain Bolt

QUESTION

Marja-Liisa Kirvesniemi (Finland) competed in six different Winter Olympic Games in what event?

> **ANSWER**
>
> Skiing

QUESTION

Teofilo Stevenson (Cuba) won three Olympic gold medals in boxing and famously turned down $5 million to fight what other boxer?

ANSWER

Muhammad Ali

QUESTION

In 1952, Emil Zatopek of Czechoslovakia became the only person to win the 5,000-meter race, the 10,000-meter race, and what other event in the same Olympics?

ANSWER

The marathon

QUESTION

The first winter Olympics were held in 1924 in what country?

ANSWER

France

QUESTION

In what year were women first permitted to compete in the Olympics?

ANSWER

1900

QUESTION

Lauryn Williams became the first American woman to win Olympic medals in both the Summer and Winter games, after claiming silver in track and field and what winter sport?

ANSWER

Bobsled

QUESTION

All-around athlete Lottie Dod was the youngest ever Wimbledon winner at 15 years old in 1887. She also won the Amateur British Open in golf, and a silver medal in the 1908 Olympics in what sport?

ANSWER

Archery
(As if that wasn't enough,
she also played for England's
national field hockey team.)

QUESTION

At the 2008 Olympics, American Michael Phelps broke whose record for most gold medals in swimming?

ANSWER

Mark Spitz

BONUS Round!

BONUS Round!

Through 2022, the Olympics canceled were canceled four times.
Name the years they were canceled.
You may take four total guesses.
(One point per correct answer for a maximum of 4 points.)

1916

1940

1944

2020

QUESTION

Through 2022,
which country has hosted the
most Olympic Games?

ANSWER

United States

QUESTION

In 2016, which sport made the Olympic roster for the first time since 1924?

ANSWER

Rugby

QUESTION

After finishing a disappointing 8th in the 50-meter speed skating event at the 1984 Olympics, what American speed skater returned to win gold in that event at the next three Olympics?

ANSWER

Bonnie Blair

QUESTION

How old was skier Lindsey Vonn (United States) when she made her Olympic debut?

ANSWER

17

QUESTION

Which city hosted the first boycott-free Olympics since 1972?

> **ANSWER**
>
> Barcelona (1992)

QUESTION

At the 1924 Olympics, runner Paavo Nurmi (Finland) made history by becoming the first athlete ever to win how many gold medals in a single Olympic Games?

ANSWER

Five

QUESTION

Karin Buttner-Janz (Germany) won gold on the uneven bars at the 1972 Olympics, defeating what gymnast who was favored to win the event?

ANSWER

Olga Korbut

QUESTION

On "Saturday Night Live," John Belushi famously parodied what athlete for waving a small American flag after smashing the world record in the decathlon at the 1976 Olympics?

ANSWER

Bruce Jenner

BONUS Round!

BONUS Round!

Below are five questions about figure skating at the Olympics. Read them one at a time. The guesser may take one guess per question. (One point for each correct answer for a maximum of 5 points.)

Sonja Henie won more Olympic titles (three) than any other female figure skater. What country did she represent?	**Norway**
This figure skater won silver at the 1994 Games after surviving a physical attack orchestrated by a rival.	**Nancy Kerrigan**
She was the first Korean figure skater to win Olympic gold, and through 2022, held the record for highest score at the Olympics.	**Yuna Kim**
Chinese skater Zhang Min landed the first clean quadruple jump in Olympic competition in this year.	**1994**
She was the first female figure skater to land a triple Axel at the Olympics.	**Midori Ito**

QUESTION

What Australian nicknamed "The Thorpedo" won nine Olympic medals in swimming?

ANSWER

Ian Thorpe

QUESTION

Claressa Shield became
the first boxer, male or female,
to accomplish what
Olympic feat?

ANSWER

She won gold medals in back-to-back Olympics. (Women's middleweight division in 2012 and 2016)

QUESTION

True or false: The longest wrestling match in Olympic history last seven hours.

ANSWER

False. It lasted 11 hours and 40 minutes and took place at the 1912 Olympics.

1 POINT

QUESTION

True or false: The first known Olympic Games were held in the early 1500s.

ANSWER

False.
They were held in 776 B.C.

QUESTION

George Eyser (United States) won six medals in this sport at the 1904 Olympics while competing with a wooden leg.

ANSWER

Gymnastics
(He lost his leg after getting run over by a train as a child.)

QUESTION

In what year were the Summer Olympics first televised live?

ANSWER

1936

QUESTION

How many Olympic gold medals does U.S. tennis star Serena Williams have?

ANSWER

Four

QUESTION

What Olympian was voted as the greatest female athlete of the 20th century by "Sports Illustrated" in 2000?

ANSWER

Jackie Joyner-Kersee
(United States)

QUESTION

Who is the only gymnast ever to compete in eight Olympic Games?

ANSWER

Oksana Chusovitina (She competed for the Unified Team in 1992, Uzbekistan in 1996, 2000, 2004, 2016 and 2021, and Germany in 2008 and 2012.)

Which sport was dropped from the Olympic program after the 1936 Berlin Games?

ANSWER
Polo

BONUS Round!

BONUS Round!

Through 2022, five countries have had all of their Olympic medals won by female athletes. Name the five countries.
You may take five total guesses.
(Two points for each correct answer for a maximum of 10 points.)

Zimbabwe (8 medals)

Bahrain (4 medals)

Costa Rica (4 medals)

Mozambique (2 medals)

Montenegro (1 medal)

QUESTION

How many countries boycotted the 1980 Moscow Olympics?

ANSWER

66

QUESTION

How old was the oldest Olympic medal winner?

ANSWER

72 years old
(Oscar Swahn of Sweden
won silver in the double shot
running deer contest in 1920.)

QUESTION

Which Olympic gymnast was awarded the first-ever perfect 10 on the uneven bars?

ANSWER

Nadia Comaneci (Romania)

QUESTION

Nicknamed "The Flying Housewife," Dutch track and field star Fanny Blankers-Koen became the first woman to win this number of gold medals at a single Olympic Games (1984).

ANSWER

Four
(In her career, she set world records in eight different events.)

2 POINTS

QUESTION

What is the maximum weight for a men's boxing heavyweight in the Olympics?

ANSWER

There is no maximum weight.

QUESTION

The three Olympic values are Excellence, Friendship and what?

ANSWER

Respect

QUESTION

True or false: Ancient Olympic Games lasted five or six months.

ANSWER

True!

QUESTION

True or false: The Olympic Torch has been carried into space several times.

ANSWER

True!
(It was unlit.)

QUESTION

Through 2022, which Olympic Games were the most expensive to produce, at $22 billion?

> ANSWER

2014 Sochi Winter Olympics

QUESTION

The 1980 Winter Olympics held in Lake Placid, New York, were the first to use what for winter events?

ANSWER

Artificial snow

QUESTION

What kind of dog was the first official Olympic mascot?

ANSWER

Dachshund

QUESTION

The United States and the Soviet Union are first and second for the countries with most Olympic medals overall. What country is in third place for overall number of medals?

ANSWER

Great Britain

QUESTION

How many players are on the field for each team in an Olympic soccer match?

ANSWER

11

QUESTION

In 1960, the ninth International Stoke Mandeville Games took place and were also considered to be the first what?

ANSWER

Paralympic Games

QUESTION

At 41, this U.S. athlete became the oldest swimmer to ever compete in the Olympics.

ANSWER

Dara Torres
(She won three silver medals at her fifth and final Olympics in 2008, and 12 medals overall.)

QUESTION

True or false: At the ancient Olympics held in Greece, women were not allowed to be spectators.

ANSWER

True!

QUESTION

True or false:
1912 was the last year when Olympic gold medals were made entirely of gold.

ANSWER

True!
(Olympic gold medals are now
made mostly of silver.)

QUESTION

In what year did snowboarding make its Olympic debut?

ANSWER

1998

QUESTION

What athlete has the most Olympic medals for any woman in any sport, and is second only to Michael Phelps on the all-time list?

ANSWER

Larisa Latynina
(Soviet Union)

QUESTION

Which was the first Latin American city to host the Olympics?

ANSWER

Mexico City

QUESTION

The Winter and Summer Olympics were held separately starting in what year?

ANSWER

1994

QUESTION

Who was the youngest champion ever in the Winter Olympics?

ANSWER

Tara Lipinski
(American figure skater)

QUESTION

Which sport returned to the Olympics in 2016 after a 112-year absence?

ANSWER

Golf

QUESTION

In 1896, Spiridon Louis became the first athlete to win what Olympic event?

ANSWER

The marathon

QUESTION

One of the mascots for the 2000 Olympics was named Syd and was what kind of animal?

> ANSWER

A duck billed platypus

QUESTION

What country has the highest number of Olympic medals without ever winning a gold?

ANSWER

Malaysia
(13 medals total)

QUESTION

Which event is the last event in the Olympic Decathlon?

ANSWER

1,500-meter run

BONUS Round!

BONUS Round!

UP TO 10 POINTS

The 1992 United States men's Olympic basketball team, nicknamed the "Dream Team," was the first American Olympic team to feature active players from the NBA. The team won gold, and has been described as the greatest sports team ever assembled.
Name the 12 players on the team. You may take 12 total guesses.
(One point per correct answer.
A maximum of 10 points only for this bonus round.)

Earvin 'Magic' Johnson
Michael Jordan
Larry Bird
David Robinson
Patrick Ewing
Karl Malone
Charles Barkley
John Stockton
Scottie Pippen
Christian Laettner
Clyde Drexler
Chris Mullin

QUESTION

At 4 feet and 8 inches, she was the shortest American athlete at the 2016 Rio Olympics.

ANSWER

Simone Biles (gymnastics)

QUESTION

In which year did the sport of table tennis make its Olympic debut?

ANSWER

1988

QUESTION

During the Ancient Olympics, wrestlers covered their bodies with what?

ANSWER

Oil

QUESTION

Iraq won its only Olympic medal in 1960 for what sport?

ANSWER

Weightlifting

QUESTION

Through 2022, which is the only city to have been awarded the Summer Olympics three times?

ANSWER

London, England

QUESTION

What Olympic figure skating team got perfect scores for their interpretation of Maurice Ravel's "Bolero?"

ANSWER

Jayne Torvill and Christopher Dean

QUESTION

Which Olympic sport is played with stones and brooms?

ANSWER

Curling

QUESTION

Through 2022, which country has the most gold medals at the Winter Olympics?

ANSWER

Norway

QUESTION

In which sport did India win its first ever gold medal at the Olympics?

ANSWER

Men's field hockey

QUESTION

American Al Oerter won gold at four consecutive Olympics (1956-1968) in what track and field event?

ANSWER

Discus throw

BONUS Round!

BONUS Round!

Only five countries have been represented at every modern-era Summer Olympic Games. Name them.
Your may take five guesses total.
(One point for each correct answer for a maximum of 5 points.)

Greece

Great Britain

France

Switzerland

Australia

QUESTION

Olympic equestrian events are divided into three disciplines: dressage, eventing, and what?

ANSWER

Jumping

QUESTION

Through 2022, which country has won the most medals in swimming?

ANSWER

United States

QUESTION

What was the original prize for athletes who won in the Ancient Olympics?

ANSWER

An olive wreath crown

QUESTION

Clara Hughes is the first person, male or female, to win multiple medals at both the Summer and Winter Olympics. What country did she represent?

ANSWER

Canada
(She competed in cycling and speed skating.)

QUESTION

Through 2022, how many Olympic Games have taken place in Africa?

ANSWER

Zero

QUESTION

Who was the first Olympic athlete to be disqualified for testing positive for steroids?

ANSWER

Ben Johnson
(United States)

QUESTION

In what year did the Torch Relay make its Olympic debut?

ANSWER

1936

QUESTION

To mark the end of the first Olympic Games, the ancient Greeks slaughtered what animal?

ANSWER

Ox

QUESTION

Which Olympiac champion was also a winner of "The Masked Dancer"?

ANSWER

Gabby Douglas
(United States gymnast)

QUESTION

What Olympic sport uses a piece of equipment called a foil?

ANSWER

Fencing

QUESTION

Which U.S. city was the first to host the modern Olympics?

ANSWER

St. Louis, Missouri

QUESTION

Which historical explorer's route was followed by the Olympic Torch Relay in 1968?

> **ANSWER**

Christopher Columbus

QUESTION

Babe Didrikson is the only athlete, male or female, to win individual Olympic medals in three separate track and field categories. She won the 80-meter hurdle (running), javelin (throwing), and what other event?

ANSWER

High jump (jumping)

QUESTION

After a tie for second place occurred at the 1936 Olympics, the silver and bronze medals were cut and in half. They were then fused together to make two medals that were each half-silver and half-bronze. In what sport did this tie occur?

ANSWER

Pole vaulting

POINTS

QUESTION

What gymnast became well-known for her smirk at the Olympics and later appeared in a commercial for GEICO because of it?

ANSWER

McKayla Maroney
(United States)

QUESTION

In which city did Muhammad Ali light the Olympic Cauldron?

ANSWER

Atlanta, Georgia

QUESTION

The four types of swimming strokes in the Olympics are butterfly, backstroke, breaststroke and what?

ANSWER

Freestyle

QUESTION

What simple game involving a rope was part of the Olympics until 1920?

ANSWER

Tug-of-War

QUESTION

Where is the Olympic Flame lit annually?

ANSWER

Olympia, Greece

QUESTION

What do white doves represent when released at the Olympic Opening Ceremony?

Peace

Thank you!

The purchase of this book supported a small business. We hope you enjoyed it!

Printed in Great Britain
by Amazon